Stone Pizza

by Liza Charlesworth
illustrated by Jim Paillot

■SCHOLASTIC

New York ★ Toronto ★ London ★ Auckland
Sydney ★ Mexico City ★ New Delhi ★ Hong Kong

To an
incredible kid named
Noah Imani

ISBN 978-0-545-68633-4

Copyright © 2011 by Lefty's Editorial Services

All rights reserved. Published by Scholastic Inc.
SCHOLASTIC, LET'S LEARN READERS™, and associated logos are trademarks and/or registered trademarks of Scholastic Inc.

12 11 10 9 8 7 6 5 4 3 2 1   14 15 16 17 18 19/0

Printed in China.

Once upon a time, there was a place called Myville. It was a tiny town with a big problem: The people who lived there did not share.

They did not share their toys or tools or food. A boy with a bat lived next to a girl with a ball. But they never played baseball. A man with peanut butter lived next to a woman with jelly. But they never made peanut butter and jelly sandwiches.

One day, a poor pizza maker named
Tony Pepperoni rode into Myville on his trusty
mule. Tony had been traveling a long time.
He was very hungry. So he asked the people
if they would share some food.

"No, no, no!" they replied.

But Tony was not discouraged.

"That's all right," he said. "I can still make the best pizza in the world."

Tony went to the center of town. First, he built a fire. Then he found the perfect stone. It was big and round and flat as a pancake.

"Mama Mia, from this bit of granite,

I'll make the best pizza on the whole planet!" he sang.

By and by, a man carrying some flour walked past.

"What are you doing?" he asked.

"I'm making stone pizza," said Tony.

"Yuck," said the man. "That sounds awful!"

"No! It's the best pizza on the planet," replied Tony. "But a little of your flour would make it even better."

Then Tony sang:

"Mama Mia, my pizza's sooooo nice,

If you choose to share, you get a slice."

The man did not want to share. But he did want a slice of the best pizza on the planet. So he gave Tony some flour.

"Thanks," said Tony. He used the flour to make dough. He pounded it into a big circle. Then he put it on top of the stone to bake.

By and by, a lady carrying some tomatoes walked past.

"What are you doing?" she asked.

"I'm making stone pizza," Tony said.

"Ick," she said. "That sounds horrible!"

"No! It's the best pizza on the planet," he replied. "But a few of your tomatoes would make it even better."

Then Tony sang:

"Mama Mia, my pizza's sooooo nice,

If you choose to share, you get a slice."

The lady did not want to share. But she did want a slice of the best pizza on the planet. So she handed Tony some tomatoes.

"Thanks," said Tony. He used the tomatoes
to make a sauce. *Splish! Splash!* He poured the
sauce on the dough.

The pizza began to bubble and bake. *Mmmm!* One by one, the people of Myville came to see what smelled so good. Tony told everyone about his stone pizza. And he convinced each person to add something to it.

A boy shared some cheese. A girl shared some meatballs.

A couple shared their juicy pineapple and super-sour pickles.

Before long, everyone in the town had shared something—even the mayor of Myville himself! He added his whole jelly bean collection.

The stone pizza bubbled and baked. It smelled more delicious with each passing minute. At last, it was done. Tony sang:

"Mama Mia, from this bit of granite,
I made the best pizza on the whole planet!"

Tony gave big slices to all the folks in town.
"Fabulous!" said the man who shared the flour.
"Perfect!" said the lady who shared the pickles.
Everyone agreed that it was the yummiest pizza
they had ever tasted.

"Tony, how did you make such a scrumptious pizza?" asked the mayor.

"When you have a stone and people who share, anything is possible!" replied the wise pizza maker with a wink.

The mayor was delighted with everyone's generosity. So he changed the name of the town from Myville to Ourville. And from that day on, folks shared everything they had.

Tony Pepperoni decided to stay in Ourville and open up a pizzeria. The pizzeria became world famous and everyone lived—and shared—happily ever after.

Comprehension Boosters

1. Retell this story in your own words.

2. Why did the man with the flour decide to share some with Tony?

3. Why did the mayor change the name of the town from *Myville* to *Ourville*?

4. Can you think of five great words to describe Tony's stone pizza?

5. What happens *after* everyone lives happily ever after? Turn on your imagination and tell a story about it!